NICHOLAS NICKLEBY

by Charles Dickens

Adapted by Steve Barlow and Steve Skidmore

Illustrated by
Annabel Spenceley

Series Editors
Steve Barlow and Steve Skidmore

Nicholas Nickleby

This play is adapted from part of *Nicholas Nickleby*, a novel written by Charles Dickens in 1839.

Nicholas Nickleby's father has died, and in order to try to make a living, Nicholas is persuaded by his Uncle Ralph to apply for a job as an assistant schoolteacher at Dotheboys (pronounced 'Do-the-boys') Hall, run by Mr Wackford Squeers and his wife.

Fanny Squeers

The Characters

Nicholas Nickleby
A young man.

Mr Wackford Squeers
The headmaster of Dotheboys Hall. He is a monstrous bully.

Mrs Squeers
Mr Squeers' wife. She is as bad as her husband!

Smike
A 19 year-old pupil at the school. He is always being picked on by Mr and Mrs Squeers.

Fanny Squeers
Mr and Mrs Squeers' daughter.

Young Wackford Squeers
Mr and Mrs Squeers' son.

Tilda Price
Fanny Squeers' best friend.

Mr Snawley
The stepfather of two new pupils.

Belling
A new pupil at the school.

Tavern Waiter

Boy
A pupil.

Bolder
A pupil.

Tompkins
A pupil.

Non-speaking parts
Graymarsh, Mobbs, Cobbey and other boys at the school.

Mrs Squeers

Tilda Price

Young Wackford
Squeers

Nicholas
Nickleby

Mr Wackford
Squeers

Smike

Mr Squeers: *(Looking at his watch)* Half-past three. There will be nobody here today. Last term I took ten boys down to the school. At twenty pound a head. Two hundred pound. I go back tomorrow morning and all I've got is three. Three twenties is sixty pound. What's happened to all the boys?

Belling: *(Sneezing)* Achoo!

Mr Squeers: What's that, Belling?

Belling: *(Scared)* Please, sir, I sneezed.

Mr Squeers: Oh, you sneezed, did you?

(Belling begins to cry. Mr Squeers knocks him off the trunk with a blow.)

Mr Squeers: Wait 'til I get you to Yorkshire, my young gentleman, and then I'll give you the rest. Will you stop that noise?

Belling: *(Crying)* Ye- ye- yes.

Mr Squeers: Then do so at once.

(A waiter enters.)

Waiter: Mr Squeers, there's a gentleman to see you.

Mr Squeers: Send him in.

(The waiter exits. Mr Squeers turns to Belling.)

Mr Squeers: *(Whispering nastily)* Put your handkerchief in your pocket, or I'll murder you when the gentleman goes.

(Nicholas Nickleby enters.)

Nicholas: Mr Squeers?

Mr Squeers: The same.

Nicholas: My name is Nicholas Nickleby.

Mr Squeers: Delighted, I'm sure. How may I help you, Mr Nickleby? Never postpone business, I say. Indeed, it is the very first lesson we teach our pupils. Master Belling, my dear, always remember that, do you hear?

Belling: Yes, sir.

Mr Squeers:	What must we never do, Master Belling?
Belling:	Never ... *(He desperately tries to remember.)*
Mr Squeers:	Very good indeed. Go on.
Nicholas:	*(Helpfully)* P ...
Belling:	Perform ... business. Never perform business!
Mr Squeers:	*(Hissing nastily into Belling's ear)* You and I will perform some business with the end of my belt when the gentleman has gone!
Nicholas:	Mr Squeers, sir, I believe you have advertised for an assistant schoolteacher. Well, here I am! My uncle, Mr Ralph Nickleby, gave me a letter of introduction to you.
	(Nicholas holds out a letter to Mr Squeers, who looks at it with disgust.)
Mr Squeers:	You mean ... you haven't any boys?
Nicholas:	*I?* Good heavens, no.
Mr Squeers:	You are not, in fact, a parent?
Nicholas:	No, sir.
	(The waiter enters.)

Waiter:	Another gentleman to see you, sir.
Mr Squeers:	Alone?
Waiter:	He has two boys with him.
Mr Squeers:	The day gets better! Send them in!
	(The waiter exits.)
Mr Squeers:	*(To Belling)* No snivelling, or else!
	(Snawley and his two boys enter. Mr Squeers' manner changes at once.)
Mr Squeers:	*(As sweetly as can be)* My dear child, don't cry. Don't worry. You are leaving your friends, but you will have a father in me and a mother in Mrs Squeers. At the delightful school of Dotheboys Hall near Great Bridge in Yorkshire, where children are boarded, clothed, washed, given pocket money and provided with all the comforts of home ...
Snawley:	Er, Mr Wackford Squeers, the headmaster of Dotheboys Hall School?
	(Mr Squeers turns round, pretending to be surprised at Mr Snawley's entrance.)
Mr Squeers:	I am the same, sir.
Snawley:	My name is Snawley.
Mr Squeers:	A remarkably pretty name.

Snawley: *(Pointing at the two boys)* I have been thinking of placing my two boys at your school.

Mr Squeers: You couldn't place them anywhere better, sir! Every home comfort that a boy could wish for will be theirs.

Snawley: I want their morals to be particularly attended to. You are a moral man?

Mr Squeers: I believe I am, sir.

Nicholas: *(Who has been trying to attract Mr Squeers' attention)* Sir, the position?

Mr Squeers: I am afraid you won't suit me, Mister Nickleby.

Nicholas: Do you think I am too young, or is it because I do not have a degree?

Mr Squeers: *(With an eye on Snawley)* The lack of a college degree is a problem.

Snawley: Mr Squeers, can I speak to you in private?

(Mr Squeers nods and Mr Snawley moves him away from Nicholas, the two boys and Belling.)

Snawley: Up to what age do you keep boys at your school?

Mr Squeers: For as long as as their friends make the payment of twenty pounds per year or until they run away!

Snawley: I see.

(Mr Squeers glances at Nicholas and draws Snawley further out of earshot.)

Mr Squeers: Let us understand one another. These two boys you've brought here ... ?

Snawley: I'm their stepfather.

Mr Squeers: So that's it! I wondered why you wanted to send them to Yorkshire. We have many such boys at the school.

Snawley: I married their mother and she has little money. If we kept them at home, she'd waste it by spending it all on them, and spoil them something terrible.

Mr Squeers: I see.

Snawley: So I wish to send them to a school a long way away, where there are no holidays, no coming home and no comforts. Do you understand?

Mr Squeers: Payments regular and no questions asked.

Snawley: *(Hopefully)* There's not too much writing home allowed?

Mr Squeers: None, except a circular at Christmas to say that they are very happy and hope they never have to come home.

Snawley: Excellent. We understand each other.

(He takes out a purse with coins in it and presses it into Mr Squeers' hand.)

Mr Squeers: We do. *(He shakes Snawley's hand.)*

Nicholas: Please read my uncle's letter, sir.

(Mr Squeers snatches the letter crossly from Nicholas' hand, takes it out of the envelope and reads it.)

Nicholas: You see, sir, my father is dead. I am looking for a position so that I may provide for my mother and sister. My uncle says that by teaching at your school, I shall be setting out on the road to my fortune.

(During Nicholas' speech, Mr Squeers looks more closely at the envelope, and then shakes it. It rattles. Turning to Snawley so that Nicholas cannot see what he is doing, Squeers tips some coins out of the envelope, bites one and puts the coins in his pocket. He exchanges a wink with Snawley and turns a beaming face to Nicholas.)

Mr Squeers: Well, Mr Nickleby, your uncle has persuaded me!

(Nicholas shakes Mr Squeers' hand joyfully.)

Nicholas: ·Oh, thank you, sir.

Mr Squeers: We leave tomorrow morning by coach, Nickleby. Eight o'clock sharp. Mr Snawley, you may with every confidence leave your precious boys in the loving and safe hands of Mr Wackford Squeers and his new assistant teacher!

Mr Squeers: Here we are, then. Dotheboys Hall! Mind you, it isn't really a hall.

Nicholas: Oh, really, sir?

Mr Squeers: I call it a hall in London because it sounds better. A man may call his house an island, there's no law against it. Now, where's Smike? Smike! Smike!

(Smike rushes in. Mr Squeers hits him.)

Mr Squeers: Why the devil didn't you greet us at the door?

Smike: Please, sir, I fell asleep at the fire.

Mr Squeers: Fire, what fire? Where is there a fire?

Smike: Only in the kitchen. Missus said as I was up I might go in there for a warm.

Mr Squeers: Missus is a fool. You'd have been more awake if you were cold. Take care of these bags and then get the boys in here.

(Smike takes the bags and exits. Mrs Squeers, Fanny Squeers and Young Wackford Squeers enter.)

Mrs Squeers: Oh, my Squeery! *(She gives him a back-breaking hug.)*

Mr Squeers:	My love! And how have the cows been keeping while I've been away?
Mrs Squeers:	All right, every one of them.
Mr Squeers:	And the pigs?
Mrs Squeers:	As well as they were when you went away.
Mr Squeers:	And the boys?
Mrs Squeers:	Oh, they're well enough; except that young Pitcher's had a fever.
Mr Squeers:	Drat the boy! He's always doing something of that sort. *(He realizes that Mrs Squeers has just noticed Nicholas.)* This is the new young man, my dear.
Mrs Squeers:	Oh.
Mr Squeers:	Mr Nickleby, my wife Mrs Squeers, my daughter Miss Squeers and my son, young Wackford Squeers. *(Fanny giggles. Young Wackford just glares at Nicholas.)*
Mr Squeers:	Call the boys down, Wackford, and if they don't hurry you know how to quicken them along.
Young Wackford:	Yes, Father! *(He picks up a cane and exits.)*
Mr Squeers:	He is a fine young man, who takes after me. *(Nicholas looks in amazement at Mr Squeers.)*

Young Wackford: *(Offstage)* Come on, you lazybones!

(There is the sound of thrashing and the schoolboys, including Smike, enter, crying out in pain and rubbing their heads, backsides and legs. They are closely followed by Young Wackford.)

Mr Squeers: Sit down! Quickly!

(The boys sit in rows to listen to Mr Squeers.)

Mr Squeers: If any boy speaks without permission, I'll take the skin off his back. Understand?

Boys: Yes, sir, Mr Squeers, sir.

Mr Squeers: Boys, I've been to London and have returned to my family and you as strong and as well as ever.

Mrs Squeers: Three cheers, boys. Hip, hip ...

Boys: *(Half-heartedly)* Hooray.

Mrs Squeers: *(Staring daggers at the boys)* I said 'Hip, hip ...'

Boys: Hooray.

(She begins to hit at the boys with a cane.)

Mrs Squeers: HIP, HIP!

Boys: *(As loudly as possible)* HOORAY!

Mr Squeers: Thank you for that kind greeting. I wish to introduce you to a new teacher, Mr Nickleby. I'm sure that you will grow to love him, just as much as you love myself and Mrs Squeers.

(The boys mutter to themselves.)

Mr Squeers: Silence! *(He waves his cane in the air.)* Now, I have had letters from some of your parents, and they're so pleased with your progress that they want you to stay here as long as possible. Which is pleasing for everyone.

(One or two of the boys begin to sniffle and cry at this news.)

Mr Squeers: But I also have some disappointing news. Where is Bolder?

(Bolder puts his hand up.)

Mr Squeers: Your father was two pounds ten shillings short in his payment. Come here, Bolder.

(Bolder moves to Mr Squeers.)

Mr Squeers: Bolder, you are a no-good rascal. As the last thrashing seems to have done you no good, we'll have to see if another one will beat the bad out of you!

(Mr Squeers sets about Bolder, hitting him with the cane. He finally stops, leaving Bolder crying with pain.)

Mr Squeers: Let's see if that works! And stop that noise. Put him outside, Smike!

(Smike leads the crying Bolder out.)

Mr Squeers: Now, let us see. A letter for Cobbey. Stand up, Cobbey.

(Cobbey stands up. Mr Squeers hands the letter to Mrs Squeers.)

Mrs Squeers: Oh! Cobbey's grandmother is dead and his Uncle John has taken to drinking. That's all the news your sister sends, except for eighteen pence, which will pay for that broken square of glass.

Mr Squeers: Sit down, Cobbey.

*(Cobbey sits down, looking miserable.
Mrs Squeers takes the coins and puts them in her
pocket. Mr Squeers hands another letter to Mrs
Squeers.)*

Mr Squeers: Graymarsh! *(Graymarsh stands up.)*

Mrs Squeers: Graymarsh's aunt is very glad to hear that he is well and happy and she thinks Mrs Squeers must be an angel and Mr Squeers is too good for this world. She would have sent some socks, but has no money. She hopes Graymarsh will put his trust in God, and that he will not object to sleeping five in a bed.

Mr Squeers: *(Handing Mrs Squeers another letter)* Mobbs!

(Mobbs stands as Graymarsh sits.)

Mrs Squeers: Mobbs' stepmother has become ill, since she heard that Mobbs refuses to eat fat and turns his nose up at cow's liver broth. She hopes that Mr Squeers will flog Mobbs into a happier state of mind.

Mr Squeers: Mobbs, come here!

(Mobbs moves slowly to Mr Squeers.)

Mr Squeers: Being unhappy isn't good enough. You must be cheerful!

(He beats Mobbs. Mobbs leaves the room, crying.)

Mr Squeers: There are more letters with money in, but
Mrs Squeers will take care of all that, won't you,
my dear?

Mrs Squeers: Yes, my dear.

Mr Squeers: Off to bed with you, then!

*(The boys hurriedly leave the room, beaten as they go
by Young Wackford.)*

Mr Squeers: Well now, we must find somewhere for my new
assistant to sleep. Let me see, who have we got
in Brooks' bed?

Mrs Squeers: In Brooks' bed ... there's Jennings, Bolder,
Graymarsh and little what's-his-name.

Mr Squeers: Ah, Brooks' is full, then. We'll find you a place
tomorrow, Nickleby; you can pull a couple of
chairs together in here for tonight, I suppose.
Up at seven to break the ice in the bucket for the
morning wash, or if the pump's froze you'll have
to make do with a dry polish.

*(The Squeers family turns to go. Squeers turns back
to speak.)*

Mr Squeers: Oh, and Nickleby ... welcome to Dotheboys Hall.

*(He laughs. He and his family go out. Fanny pauses
at the door to smile sweetly at Nicholas. Nicholas sits
down and holds his head in his hands.)*

Scene 3
The schoolroom. Next morning.
Enter Mrs Squeers. She sniffs at a large, bubbling pan and makes a face (it's very nasty!) Then she looks around for something as Mr Squeers and Nicholas enter.

Mrs Squeers: Drat the thing! I can't find the school spoon anywhere.

Mr Squeers: Never mind, dear, it doesn't matter.

Mrs Squeers: Of course it does! It's brimstone morning!

Mr Squeers: I forgot, my dear! Of course it is! *(To Nicholas)* We purify the boys' blood now and then, Nickleby.

Mrs Squeers:	Fiddlesticks, my dear. We give them brimstone and treacle for two reasons. First, because if we didn't give them something in the way of medicine they'd always be ill and giving us trouble. Secondly, because it spoils their appetite for the whole day, and it's cheaper than giving them food at breakfast or dinner. So it does them good and it does us good, and that's fair enough.
Nicholas:	*(Shocked)* Indeed.
Mrs Squeers:	Drat it! Where *is* the blessed thing? Smike! Where are you?

(Smike enters.)

Mrs Squeers:	Where is the school spoon, Smike?
Smike:	I don't know, Mrs Squeers.
Mrs Squeers:	*(Hitting Smike)* Don't know? Don't know?
Mr Squeers:	He's probably lost it, my dear.

(Mrs Squeers continues to hit Smike. Nicholas looks on in disgust.)

Mrs Squeers:	Where is it?
Smike:	Is it in your pocket, Mrs Squeers?
Mrs Squeers:	In my pocket? In my pocket?

(She hits Smike again.)

Mr Squeers:	How dare you answer back, Smike!

(Mr Squeers hits Smike.)

Smike: I only thought ...

Mrs Squeers: In my pocket! What a ridiculous idea! In my pocket!

(Mrs Squeers hits Smike again.)

Mrs Squeers: *(Fumbling in her pocket)* As if it could be, as if it could be ...

(She pauses and brings out the spoon from her pocket.)

Mrs Squeers: In my pocket! Of course it was! I knew it was there all the time. *(To Smike)* Why didn't you tell me it was in my pocket?

Smike: But I ...

Mrs Squeers: *(Hitting him again)* Be quiet! And be more respectful in future.

Smike: Sorry, ma'am.

(Smike, still crying from the beating, lifts the lid off the pan of brimstone and treacle. Mrs Squeers stands over it with her spoon.)

Mrs Squeers: Now, Mr Squeers. I am ready! Call the boys.

Mr Squeers: *(Shouting)* Boys! Down here straight away!

(The boys enter.)

Mr Squeers: Line up! Time for your medicine!

(The boys form a line. They move forward one at a time to Mrs Squeers and the brimstone.)

Mrs Squeers: Smike! Open wide!

(She gives Smike a spoonful.)

Smike: Urghh!

(Smike staggers away with his hand over his mouth.)

Mrs Squeers: Next!

(This continues until all the boys have had their brimstone and treacle. As they wait, Mr Squeers turns to Nicholas in great satisfaction.)

Mr Squeers: A wonderful woman, my wife, Nickleby.

Nicholas: (*Sarcastically*) Indeed.

Mr Squeers: I don't know anyone like her.

Nicholas: Nor do I.

Mr Squeers: She's a mother to these boys, Nickleby. In fact, she's more than a mother. She does things for these boys that no mother would ever do.

Nicholas: (*Looking at Smike*) I agree wholeheartedly with you.

(*The last boy takes his medicine and staggers, coughing, back to his place.*)

Mrs Squeers: Have you all had your medicine?

Boys: Yes, ma'am, Mrs Squeers, ma'am.

Mrs Squeers: Then bow your heads. For what we have received, may the Lord make us truly thankful!

Mr Squeers: Thank you, my dear. Now it's time for lessons. Get ready.

(*The boys set out benches and tables and sit in small groups. Unseen by Mr Squeers or Nicholas, Fanny Squeers and Mrs Squeers watch from the doorway.*)

Mr Squeers: This is the first class in English spelling and philosophy, Nickleby. Now then, where's the first boy?

Boy: Please, sir, he's cleaning the back parlour window.

Mr Squeers:	So he is. *(To Nicholas)* We follow the practical way of teaching, Nickleby. C - L - E - A - N, clean. Verb. To make bright. W - I - N, win, D - E - R, der, winder, a thing for looking out of. When the boy knows how to spell it, he goes and cleans it.
Nicholas:	I see.
Mr Squeers:	Where's the second boy?
Boy:	Please, sir, he's weeding the garden.
Mr Squeers:	To be sure. So he is. G - A - R, gar, D- I - N, din, gardin, a place where plants grow. When a boy has learned that a gardin is a place where plants grow, he goes off and helps them do it. That's our system, Nickleby, what do you think of it?
Nicholas:	*(Sarcastically)* It's a very useful one.
Mr Squeers:	Third boy. What's a horse?
Boy:	A beast.
Mr Squeers:	So it is. A horse has four legs. It's a quadruped. And 'quadruped' is Latin for 'beast', as everyone that has studied grammar knows, or else what's the use of knowing grammar?
Nicholas:	What indeed?
Mr Squeers:	*(To the boy)* As you're perfect in that, go and look after my horse.
	(The boy runs off.)

Mr Squeers:	And the rest of you can go to the well and draw up water for washing day tomorrow. Off you go!

(The rest of the boys run off.)

Mr Squeers:	That's the way we do it, Nickleby.
Nicholas:	So I see.
Mr Squeers:	And a very good way it is. Now, you go and hear some of the boys reading. You must earn your keep. Idling about here won't do.

(Nicholas bows and exits. Fanny and Mrs Squeers come forward. Fanny pulls at her father's sleeve.)

Fanny Squeers:	Father, who is this Mr Nickleby?
Mr Squeers:	I'm told he's the son of a gentleman that died the other day.
Fanny Squeers:	The son of a gentleman!
Mrs Squeers:	Hmph! I don't believe a word of it.
Fanny Squeers:	Oh, he is handsome!
Mrs Squeers:	*(Disgusted)* Handsome?
Fanny Squeers:	*(Dreamily)* He has beautiful dark eyes and such a sweet smile. And his legs, not like the boys' crooked ones, but straight and strong.
Mrs Squeers:	*(Suddenly)* That's enough of that talk. Off you go! And no more looking at Mister Nickleby. *(She shoos Fanny out.)* Legs, indeed!

Nicholas: You need not fear me. Are you cold?

Smike: *(Shivering)* N-n-no.

Nicholas: You are shivering.

Smike: I am not cold. I am used to it.

Nicholas: You poor fellow!

(Smike begins to cry.)

Smike: Oh, dear. My heart will break.

Nicholas:	*(Putting his hand on Smike's shoulder to comfort him)* Hush. Be a man. How old are you?
Smike:	Nineteen.
Nicholas:	How long have you been here?
Smike:	Since I was a little child. Years of misery and beatings. All on my own. Where are they all?
Nicholas:	Who?
Smike:	My friends! What misery I have suffered!
Nicholas:	There is always hope.
Smike:	None for me. Not like my friend Dorker.
Nicholas:	What of him?
Smike:	He died. I was with him that night. When it was silent, he said he saw faces round his bed that came from his home. He said they smiled and talked to him. He died lifting his head up to kiss them. Do you hear?
Nicholas:	Yes.
Smike:	What faces will smile on me when I die? Who will talk to me in those long nights? They cannot come from home. If they did, they would frighten me because I don't know what home is and who they would be. Pain and fear, pain and fear for me, alive or dead. No hope, no hope!

(Smike exits, leaving Nicholas sitting alone.)

Scene 5

*The Squeers' family parlour in Dotheboys Hall.
Mr Squeers, Mrs Squeers and Young Wackford
Squeers are sitting round a table.*

Mr Squeers: *(To Mrs Squeers)* Well, my dear, what do you think of him?

Mrs Squeers: Think of who?

Mr Squeers: Of the young man, the new teacher – who else could I mean?

Mrs Squeers: Oh, that Knuckleboy! I hate him!

Mr Squeers: Nickleby. You're always calling things by the wrong names.

Mrs Squeers: That doesn't matter. I see them with the right eyes and that's quite enough for me. I watched him while you beat Bolder this afternoon. He looked furious! I thought he might try to stop you.

Mr Squeers: Why do you hate him, my dear?

Mrs Squeers: What's that to you? If I hate him, that's enough, isn't it?

Mr Squeers: Quite enough for him, my dear, and a great deal too much, I daresay, if he knew. I only ask from curiosity.

Mrs Squeers: Well, then, if you want to know, I'll tell you. Because he's a proud, turned-up-nosed peacock!

Mr Squeers:	But he is cheap, my dear, the young man is very cheap. Only five pounds a year.
Mrs Squeers:	But if you don't want him, he's dear.
Mr Squeers:	But we *do* want him. Then we can put on the advertisements for the school that education is by Mr Wackford Squeers and his able assistants.
Mrs Squeers:	Well? You can put that just the same if you don't have any able assistants, can't you? Oh! I've no patience with you.
Mr Squeers:	Haven't you? Now, I'll tell you what, Mrs Squeers. In this matter of having a teacher, I'll do things my way. I need an assistant until little Wackford grows up and can take charge of the school.
Young Wackford:	(*Excited*) Am I going to take charge of the school when I'm grown up, Father?
Mr Squeers:	Yes, my son.
Young Wackford:	Wonderful!
	(*He grabs Mr Squeers' cane and starts thrashing the air with it.*)
Young Wackford:	I'll give it to the boys, Father! I'll make them squeak!
	(*He continues to thrash the air. Mr and Mrs Squeers laugh and clap their hands in joy.*)

Mrs Squeers: I still think that Knuckleboy is a stuck-up monkey.

Mr Squeers: Well, suppose he is. He's as well being stuck up here in our schoolroom as anywhere else. Especially as he doesn't like it!

Mrs Squeers: I suppose you're right. I hope that it'll bring his pride down. And I'll see to it that it does! I say it again. I hate him more than poison.

Mr Squeers: Well, I don't know anyone who can show dislike better than you, dear. And, of course, you don't have to take the trouble to hide the fact.

Mrs Squeers: I don't intend to.

Mr Squeers: And if he has a touch of pride, as I think he has, I don't believe there's a woman in all England who can bring down anybody's spirit as quick as you can, my love.

(They go out, laughing.)

Smike: I can't do it.

Nicholas: Do not try.

(Smike closes the book and begins to cry.)

Nicholas: Do not cry. I cannot bear to see you cry.

Smike: They have been beating me harder than ever.

Nicholas: I know. It is because of me. I am sorry.

Smike: No, it isn't your fault. If you weren't here, I would die. They would kill me, I know they would.

Nicholas: You will do better, poor fellow, when I am gone.

Smike: Gone! Are you going?

Nicholas: I cannot say. I was speaking my thoughts out loud.

Smike: Tell me, will you go?

Nicholas: I shall probably be driven to it. Out into the wide world.

Smike: Is the world as bad and dismal as this place?

Nicholas: No. Even its worst moments are happy compared to this place.

Smike: Would I ever meet you in the world?

Nicholas: You would; and I would help you, and not bring fresh sorrow on you as I have done here.

(Mr Squeers enters. He stares at Smike, tapping his cane in his hand.)

Mr Squeers: Smike, you've got work to do.

(Smike exits, looking back at Nicholas who watches helplessly.)

Fanny Squeers: ... and I tell you, Tilda, I never saw such legs in the whole of my life!

(They both giggle.)

Tilda: Ooh, Fanny! D'you mean this young man has come all the way from London to teach at Dotheboys Hall, just so he can be near you?

Fanny Squeers: Oh, Tilda, isn't it an extraordinary thing?

Tilda: *Very* extraordinary. But what has he said to you?

Fanny Squeers: Well, nothing yet ... but if you had only seen the way he looks at me.

Tilda: Does he look at you like this? *(She gives a silly, lopsided grin.)*

Fanny Squeers: Just like that – only more genteel.

Tilda: Oh, then he is in love with you. I can't wait to see him!

32

Fanny Squeers:	He'll be here any moment now.
	(They burst into giggles. There is a knock at the door.)
Fanny Squeers:	There he is! Oh, Tilda!
Tilda:	Hush! Tell him to come in!
Fanny Squeers:	*(Faintly)* Come in.
	(Nicholas enters.)
Nicholas:	Good evening. I understand from Mr Squeers that ...
Fanny Squeers:	Oh, yes. It's all right. Father isn't here, but I'm sure you won't mind that! Mr Nickleby, this is Tilda Price.
Nicholas:	I'm very pleased to meet you, Miss Price.
Tilda:	Mr Nickleby. But please don't you two bother about me being here. Act just as though I wasn't here.
Fanny Squeers:	Tilda! I'm ashamed of you!
	(The two women burst into giggles. Nicholas is confused, and then also begins to laugh.)
Nicholas:	*(Gallantly)* Miss Squeers did not tell me that she had such a charming friend.
Fanny Squeers:	Charming? *(She glares jealously at Tilda.)*

Tilda:	Why, Mr Nickleby, you mustn't say such things to me. You'll only make Fanny jealous.
Nicholas:	Jealous? Miss Price, you can't think ...
Tilda:	Oh, I don't think anything at all. Look at poor Fanny, dressed so beautifully and looking ... almost handsome.
Nicholas:	My dear girl, what have I got to do with her dressing beautifully or looking well?
Tilda:	Come, don't call me a dear girl, not in front of your lady!
Nicholas:	*(Alarmed)* My lady?
Tilda:	*(To Fanny who is trembling with jealousy)* Why, Fanny, my dear, I'm afraid you're not yourself today.
Fanny:	*(Hysterically)* Me? Oh, no!
Tilda:	Your hair's coming out of curl.
Fanny Squeers:	Oh, Tilda, how could you be so mean and dishonourable?
Tilda:	Why, Fanny, you're just jealous because I happen to have good enough looks for people to be polite to me. People don't make their own faces, and it's no more my fault if mine is a good one, than it is other people's fault if theirs is a bad one.
Fanny Squeers:	*(Beside herself)* Hold your tongue, or you'll make me slap you, Tilda, and afterwards I shall be sorry for it!

Nicholas: Please allow me to speak. I am very sorry that I have been the cause of any argument between you tonight.

Fanny Squeers: I forgive you!

Tilda: Have you anything else to say?

Nicholas: I fear there is something more. It is very awkward for me to say this, but does Miss Squeers think that I am in love with her?

Tilda: *(To Nicholas)* Of course she does!

Fanny Squeers: If Mr Nickleby has doubted that, he may set his mind at rest. I do love him, as he loves me ...

Nicholas: Stop! This is the greatest mistake that anyone has ever made! I have only seen Miss Squeers half a dozen times. But even if I had seen her sixty or six hundred times, my feelings would be the same. I have no intention of marrying Miss Squeers. I wish to be rid of her family and this awful place. I wish never to set foot in it again, and think of it only with loathing and disgust.

(Nicholas exits. Tilda looks shocked and Fanny bursts into tears of rage.)

Fanny Squeers: Refused! By a teacher! I hate you, Mr Nicholas Nickleby. Let him beware. I'll set Mother upon him even more! And his friend Smike! Oh, I hate everybody! I wish everybody was dead!

(She flies into a tantrum of grief and rage. Tilda tries to comfort her, really rather enjoying herself.)

Scene 8

The boys' bedroom. Nicholas enters, ringing a bell to wake the boys up. As they stagger out of their beds, Mr Squeers shouts from downstairs.

Mr Squeers:	*(Offstage)* Are you going to sleep up there all day ...
Mrs Squeers:	*(Offstage)* ... you lazy hounds?
Nicholas:	*(Shouting to Mr Squeers)* We shall be down directly, sir.
Mr Squeers:	*(Offstage)* Down directly? You had better be down directly, or I'll be down upon you! Where's that Smike?
	(There is no reply. Nicholas looks around.)
Mr Squeers:	*(Offstage)* Smike!
Mrs Squeers:	*(Offstage)* Do you want your head broke in a fresh place, Smike?
Mr Squeers:	*(Offstage)* Confound him! Nickleby!
Nicholas:	Yes, sir?

Mr Squeers: *(Offstage)* Don't you hear me calling? Send the useless lump down.

Nicholas: He is not here, sir.

Mr Squeers: *(Offstage)* Don't lie to me. He is.

Nicholas: Don't lie to *me.* He is not.

Mr Squeers: *(Offstage)* We shall soon see about that. I'll find him.

(Mr Squeers enters and rushes over to Smike's blanket. He beats the blanket, but Smike is not there.)

Mr Squeers: *(To Nicholas)* What does this mean? Where have you hid him?

Nicholas: I have seen nothing of him since last night.

Mr Squeers: Come, you won't save him this way. Where is he?

Nicholas: For all I know, he could be at the bottom of the nearest pond.

Mr Squeers: What do you mean by that? *(To the boys)* Do any of you know where Smike is?

(The boys shake their heads.)

Mr Squeers: *(Smacking his cane in his hand)* Are you sure?

(There is an uneasy silence as the boys look at each other.)

Tompkins: Please, sir, I think Smike's run away, sir.

Mr Squeers: Who said that?

Boys: Tompkins, please, sir.

(Mr Squeers grabs hold of Tompkins and brings him forward, holding him by the collar.)

Mr Squeers: And what reason do you have to think that any boy would want to run away from this establishment? Eh, sir?

Tompkins: Er ...

(Mr Squeers doesn't let him finish, but begins beating him with his cane. Tompkins rolls away, moaning and crying with pain. Nicholas is furious but cannot do anything.)

Mr Squeers:	*(To the boys)* There. Now, if any other boy thinks Smike has run away, I will be glad to have a talk with him.
	(The boys look down and shuffle their feet.)
Mr Squeers:	*(To Nicholas)* Well, Nickleby? Do *you* think he has run away?
Nicholas:	I think it extremely likely.
Mr Squeers:	Oh, you do, do you? Did he tell you he was going?
Nicholas:	He did not. And I am glad that he did not, because it would have been my duty to tell you.
Mr Squeers:	And you wouldn't have wanted to tell me, would you?
Nicholas:	No. I would not.
	(Mrs Squeers enters.)
Mrs Squeers:	What's all this to-do? *(To Mr Squeers)* Why are you talking to *him*, Squeery dear?
Mr Squeers:	Why, my dear, the fact is, Smike is not here.
Mrs Squeers:	I know that! And is there any wonder?
Mr Squeers:	Why's that, dear?

Mrs Squeers:	*(Pointing at Nicholas)* If you employ a proud teacher who makes the young dogs rebel, what do you expect? *(To Nicholas)* Now, young man, take yourself and the boys to the schoolroom. And don't you dare leave it until I tell you to, or else we will fall out in a way that will spoil your beauty.
Nicholas:	Indeed?
Mrs Squeers:	Yes, indeed and indeed again! I wouldn't keep you in this house a minute longer, if I had my way.
Nicholas:	And I wouldn't be here, if I had mine. *(To the boys)* Now, boys!
Mrs Squeers:	*(Imitating Nicholas)* Now, boys. Follow your leader, boys. *(In her normal voice)* And follow Smike's example, if you dare. You'll see what I will do to him when he gets back. And if any of you mentions his name, he'll have it twice as bad.

(Nicholas leads the boys off.)

Mr Squeers:	When I catch him, I'll beat him within an inch of his life!
Mrs Squeers:	*If* you catch him! He's run away.
Mr Squeers:	How can you be sure?
Mrs Squeers:	The cowhouse and stable are locked up, so he can't be there, and he isn't downstairs. He must have gone towards York along the public road.

Mr Squeers:	How can you be sure?
Mrs Squeers:	Stupid! He hasn't got any money, has he?
Mr Squeers:	He's never had a penny in his whole life.
Mrs Squeers:	And he didn't take anything to eat, I'm certain of that.

(Both Mr and Mrs Squeers laugh.)

Mrs Squeers:	So he will have to beg his way, and he could only do that on the public road.
Mr Squeers:	Of course!
Mrs Squeers:	Now, you take the cart and go down one road, and I'll borrow Swallow's cart and go down the other, and if we ask questions and keep our eyes open, one of us is certain to find him.
Mr Squeers:	And when we do ...

(He swishes his cane furiously.)

Scene 9

Next day. In the schoolroom. The boys are sitting at their desks. Nicholas is standing at the front of the class. Enter Mr Squeers.

Nicholas: Have you found him?

Mr Squeers: Twenty-four hours later and there's still no sign of that wretched scamp. Someone will pay if Mrs Squeers don't run him down. Mark my words. *(He looks menacingly at Nicholas and the boys.)* My pony's run right off his legs and I had to hire another horse. It cost me fifteen shillings. Who's going to pay for that?

(Nicholas shrugs his shoulders.)

Mr Squeers: I'll have it out of somebody.

(Mrs Squeers, Young Wackford and Fanny Squeers enter with Smike. He is wet and muddy. His hands have been tied.)

42

Mrs Squeers:	Here's the one to have it out of!
Mr Squeers:	Smike! Well done, my dear. Bring him here.
	(Mrs Squeers drags Smike to Mr Squeers. She unties him. Smike looks terrified.)
Mr Squeers:	Is every boy here?
	(The boys remain silent, too scared to answer back.)
Mr Squeers:	Every boy sit at his desk!
	(The boys rush to their desks.)
Mr Squeers:	Nickleby! To your desk, sir!
	(Nicholas sits at his desk.)
Mr Squeers:	Bring him here. Have you anything to say for yourself, Smike?
	(Smike shakes his head.)
Mr Squeers:	Have you anything to say?
	(Smike's head remains bowed. Mr Squeers swishes his cane in the air.)
Mr Squeers:	*(To Mrs Squeers)* Stand out of the way, Mrs Squeers, my dear. I've hardly got enough room.
Smike:	*(Pleading)* Spare me, sir!
Mr Squeers:	Oh, that's all, is it? Yes, I'll flog you within an inch of your life and spare you that!

Mrs Squeers:	*(Laughs)* That's a good 'un!
Smike:	I was driven to do it.
Mr Squeers:	Driven to do it, were you? Oh, it wasn't your fault, it was mine, I suppose, eh?
	(Mrs Squeers grabs Smike's head. As she speaks the next line, she hits him with every word.)
Mrs Squeers:	You nasty, ungrateful, pig-headed, stubborn, sneaking dog. What do you mean by that?
Mr Squeers:	Stand aside, my dear. We'll try and find out.
	(Mr Squeers grabs Smike and pulls him forward. He raises his cane and crashes it down on Smike. Smike cries out. Mr Squeers raises the cane again.)
Nicholas:	*(Shouting)* Stop!
Mr Squeers:	*(Turning round)* Who said that?
Nicholas:	I did. This must not go on.
Mr Squeers:	*(Amazed)* Must not go on?
Nicholas:	No. Must not and will not. I will prevent it.
	(Everyone in the schoolroom stares at Nicholas in amazement.)
Mr Squeers:	How dare you?
	(Mr Squeers grabs Smike again.)

Nicholas: Touch him at your peril! I will not stand by and see you beat him. My blood is up and I have the strength of ten men.

Mr Squeers: *(Pointing his cane at Nicholas)* Sit down, beggar!

Nicholas: You have insulted me many times. Your cruelty towards these boys has been terrible. If you do not stop, I will not spare you.

(Mr Squeers hits Nicholas with the cane.)

Nicholas: I warned you!

(Nicholas grabs the cane from Mr Squeers' hand and starts to hit him with it. The boys cheer him on. Mrs Squeers, Fanny Squeers and Young Wackford try to stop Nicholas. The boys try to stop them. There is chaos!)

Mr Squeers: (*Howling for mercy*) No more, I beg you!

(*With a final blow, Nicholas sends Mr Squeers spinning to the floor. He snaps the cane over his knee and throws the pieces at him. The boys cheer. The rest of the Squeers family rush to Mr Squeers' aid. Nicholas starts to walk away. Smike steps forward. He raises his hand.*)

Smike: Sir, Mr Nickleby, sir. May I go with you? I will go with you anywhere ... to the end of the world!

Nicholas: I am a friend who can do little for you.

Smike: But you are my only friend! I cannot stay here with these people. I will be your faithful, hard-working servant.

Nicholas: Then come. We shall leave this terrible place, and whatever the world has in store for us, we shall face it together.

(*As the boys cheer wildly and Mr Squeers lies groaning, Nicholas and Smike leave the stage.*)

Choosing Parts

The parts of Mr Squeers, Nicholas Nickleby, Smike, Mrs Squeers, Fanny Squeers and Tilda Price are the most demanding.

Classroom Organization

The play has been designed to enable a whole class to take part in a reading. However, it may be more appropriate for a smaller group of children to read/act out the script. There are thirteen named speaking parts, but it would be easy for confident readers to take two roles. You could read the script through with the whole class before allowing a smaller group to act out the play. Alternatively, you could ask groups of different sizes to work on different scenes, before bringing the groups back as a whole class to put the play together.

Putting On the Play

You may wish to put on a performance of the play, rather than just reading it. The following suggestions may provide you with a starting point for your own ideas about staging a production. Obviously, the use you make of these suggestions will vary depending on the time and resources available at your school.

For permission to put on a profit-making performance of *Nicholas Nickleby*, please contact the Editorial Department, Ginn & Company, Prebendal House, Parson's Fee, Aylesbury, Bucks HP20 2QY. (There is no need to apply for permission if you are not charging an entrance fee, but please let us know if you are putting on any performance of this play, as we would be interested to hear about it.)

Staging

The play is divided into nine scenes:
Scene 1 a tavern.
Scenes 2, 3, 4, 6, 9 the schoolroom at Dotheboys Hall.
Scenes 5, 7 the Squeers' family parlour.
Scene 8 the boys' bedroom.

All these locations can easily be created by arranging simple wooden benches and chairs, bringing these on and off as required. The bedroom can be suggested simply by arranging blankets on the floor of the stage. The fire mentioned in Scene 4 could be painted on to a backdrop, or a more elaborate effect could be created by placing a red light in a 'fireplace'. The Squeers' parlour should have a dining table and be decorated with ornaments to show the contrast between the Squeers' lifestyle and that of the boys.

If you have separate acting areas for the locations, the main part of the stage should be the schoolroom, the tavern could be stage right, the Squeers' family parlour stage left and the boys' bedroom on a different level, upstage centre.

Costumes

It is important to create a period feeling in a performance of *Nicholas Nickleby*. The boys should be dressed in scruffy, tattered coats and breeches. A variety of dark colours will help create the right mood.
Nicholas should be dressed in a formal frock coat as befitting a 'newly qualified teacher'!
Squeers should also be in a frock coat (perhaps shabbier than Nicholas').
Mrs Squeers should wear a long dress and an apron (with pockets).

Fanny and **Tilda** should be dressed in long dresses with shawls and various 'genteel' accompaniments.

Smike's clothes should be ill-fitting, as if he has outgrown them.

Phiz's original illustrations for *Nicholas Nickleby* will also provide inspiration for costume ideas.

Props

The following is a list of essential props:

Mr Squeers will need a cane. This can also be used by **Master Wackford** and **Mrs Squeers**.

(There are many occasions during the play when boys are hit with a cane or a hand. It is important to manage this very carefully in order to avoid injury to the children.)

Scene 1 a fob watch for **Squeers**, a travelling trunk, an envelope with coins in it.

Scene 2 travelling bags and a trunk, several letters, some with coins in them.

Scene 3 a large pan (for the brimstone), a ladle, slates for the schoolboys.

Scene 6 a book for **Smike**.

Scene 8 a handbell for **Nicholas**, blankets for the boys.

Scene 9 a rope for tying **Smike's** hands.

Follow-up Work

Research

You could encourage the children to find out more about the following:

- what happens to Nicholas and Smike when they leave Dotheboys Hall
- the life of Charles Dickens
- other stories by Dickens (television adaptations or films such as *Scrooge* or *Oliver!* can provide useful material)
- school life in Victorian times

Writing

The children could be asked to imagine that they are at Dotheboys Hall. They should write a letter to a member of their family, describing their life at Dotheboys Hall, how they are treated and what Mr Squeers and Mrs Squeers are really like.

Drama
Hot-seating

Hot-seating is a strategy which can help pupils either to create a character or to develop a greater understanding of a character in the text.

1. Put a chair at the front of the class and arrange the rest of the class in a semicircle around it.

2. Choose a child to represent one of the characters in the play, and ask him or her to sit in the hot seat.

3. The rest of the class must ask the child questions which he or she has to answer in role – in other words, as the character.

The object is to explore the characters' motivation. You could hot seat any of the main characters in this way.

4. After you have asked questions of each character, each member of the class should pronounce judgement on that character.

For example:

"You shouldn't beat the children, Mr Squeers."

"Cheer up, Smike. Nicholas will look after you."